CW00400703

For information:

E-mail: orders@branchfamilypublishing.com.

This book is printed on acid-free paper.

Printed in the United States of America.

Typesetter/Designer   Darrell Branch

Cover Designer   LJ Connell

Editor   Darrell Branch

The goal of this book is to give music creators a straightforward guide on how to transition from being a traditional beat maker to successful music producer.
Table Of Contents

www.DarrellBranch.com

Table Of Contents

Introduction

What's the difference between a beat maker and producer? That's the one million dollar question. Actually, the focus shouldn't be on deciphering the differences. The focus should be on what they have in common. A beat maker is musician who uses electrical, analog and digital instruments to create music. A producer oversees and manages the creative, recording and mixing process of a music project. As a beat maker and producer, you can perform both roles interchangeably if you acquire the necessary skills. If you're a beat maker, acquiring production skills and techniques can take you from amateur to professional music producer in no time. This is how you become a heat maker.

Heat making is the process of creating something hot, something that people can "feel." As a beat maker, you want listeners to have the same reaction about every one of your tracks. Music producers are able to replicate the process of creating "heat" by developing specific skills and techniques. Even though there isn't specific formula for making a great song, there are ten areas of focus that can help a beat maker transition to full-fledged music producer. Conceptualization, Instrumentation, Melodic Creation, Song Structure, Dynamics, Leadership, Collaboration, Mixing, Creativity and Education are all concepts that, when combined will help a beat maker develop his or her own approach and signature sound in music production.

Before we move forward, it is important that a beat maker is equipped with the foundation to put these techniques into action. To put these skills to good use, you must first have your "EEO" in order. Environment, Equipment and Organization are essential to being a heat maker. Where do you like to create music? Is your creative environment inclusive to other creators? What is your instrument of choice? Analog or digital? Software or hardware? Can you do project management? Are you able to manage your time effectively? The answers to these questions will prepare you for a future in heat making. Are you ready?

1.Conceptualization
Develop a concept/vision for your song

Most beat makers start out in much the same way. We load up our favorite drum kit, plugin, etc and begin to search for that hidden melody line or drum pattern. There is nothing wrong with this strategy at all. But, song concepts can be develop before, during or after the initial foundation of a track is created. Your goal as an aspiring producer is to be open-minded while remaining focused on the final result of your music project. One way you can maintain specific focus on the final project is by using a concept called "prosody."

Instead of adding sounds or multiple ideas, focus on how sounds and ideas will work together in unity. For example, there is a wide range of colors to choose from. If I asked you to paint a picture, you would most likely select colors that would look good together. Even with access to every color, you would only select the colors that would be pleasing to you. As a music producer, you will need to do the same with sounds. You may find this challenging at first because decisions will need to be made on what to keep in and what to leave out. This is the art of production. Listeners want to hear a unifying piece of art. One common question is "how do you know when a song is done?" If all of the elements come together to complete your vision, then you're done.

Once the initial concept or vision is developed, a producer must visualize what the final product should sound like. This includes every aspect of the song such as instrumentation, vocal production, lyrics, recordings and mixing. As the producer, it's your job to communicate you vision to all the collaborators. The concept may call for you to work with additional musicians, background singers, engineers or anyone else needed to complete the project.

Song lyrics are an essential part of any great song no matter the genre. A great melody is what

6

ultimately makes the lyrics shine though (see Melody Section). As a producer, your job is to maintain the consistency of the theme throughout the song in a creative way. The content of the lyrics should be written in a linear way that leads the listener from beginning to end. Just like a movie, the listener's instinct is build on ideas in order.

A producer must also decide in what way a song should be written. This largely depends on the style of music you are producing. As a general rule, keep the wording as simple as possible. Try using one syllable words with open vowel sounds. As I will talk about later, you don't want the lyrics to be crammed into a melody. A producer's job is to keep focus on the vision of the project throughout the production process.

2.Instrumentation
Develop musicianship that works

The term "beat making" means the process of creating music with analog and/or digital instruments. Being a musician just means you know how to play an instrument, right? Well, not exactly. Most beat makers don't consider themselves to be "traditional" musicians. In fact, being a musician isn't only about learning how to play an instrument, it's also about learning the skills to become a versatile musician. With the variety of digital instruments available on the market, much of the focus is on "how" to use and "play" the latest software or hardware device, and less of what is being played. Musicianship goes far beyond learning an instrument and playing random notes.

You probably heard phrases like, "It's not the equipment, it's how you use it" or "Its all about your ears." These are phrases that pertain to musicianship. Musicianship is a combination of skills that mold the approach to music making for musicians or beat makers. These are skills which allow you to perform your music in your own way. There are 5 areas in which a beat maker can develop skills to create his or her own form of musicianship.

The first area is called the **"External"** skill. This is a beat makers physical approach to playing his or her instrument. Do you use Midi controllers? Drum pads? Step sequencers? Computer keyboards? It's your choice. The point is, as a beat maker, you must find the appropriate controller or physical instrument that will help you create the best possible music performance. This is about comfortability, command and the flexibility of your instrument. For example, as an aspiring guitar player, you must first learn how to hold it, strum it, and position your fingers. As a beat maker, you must learn all the features available to you for your physical instrument as well. The physical attributes are the most important to focus on. If you like to play on rubber pads instead of keys, choose a unit with durable pads and the features you need.

The second area is called the **"Internal"** skill. This is a beat maker's approach to some of the traditional skills such as music theory and programming. These are technical skills that can be learned by direct instruction from educational institutions, video tutorials or self-development. Learning the basics of music theory such as reading and writing music, tempo, time signature, and key signature are essential to using music software programs. Almost every digital audio workstation is designed with the understanding that users will need to learn the basics of music theory.

The third area is called the **"Rhythmic"** skill. This is a beat maker's approach to understanding rhythm and timing. To develop rhythmic skills, one must understand note values and duration. How many times can I play each note over a period of time? A rhythm is series of note that creates a pattern. As a beat maker, you must know how to create patterns and identify specific patterns associated with music genres. These are technical skills that can be learned by direct instruction for educational institutions, video tutorials or self-development.

The fourth area is called the **"Tonal"** skill. This is a beat maker's approach to understanding melody and pitch. The foundation of western music is centered on twelve pitches. A beat maker must have knowledge of voicing , its components, scales and triads. These are technical skills that can be learned by direct instruction for educational institutions, video tutorials or self-development.

The fifth area is called the **"Creativity"** skill. This is a beat maker's approach to establishing a "X-factor." After acquiring rhythmic and tonal skills, a beat maker must develop its own unique style. These aren't technical skills that can be learned by direct instruction for educational institutions. This skill can only be developed through practice.

Beat makers spend lots of time developing their Internal and External skills. When all musicianship skills work together, a beat maker should develop the culminating skill of "audiation." Audiation is a term that refers to hearing and comprehending sounds that are not physically present. An example of audiating would be hearing a catchy melody in your head. Another example would be hearing the first part of a chord progression or melody, and in your mind, you can hear a resolution or alternate ending.

3.Melodic Creation
Create an unforgettable melody line

What is a melody? A melody is a sequence of notes that are musically satisfying. Your next question should be, what does "satisfying" mean? A satisfying melody is in the eye's of the beholder. It's all subjective. As a beat maker, you're probably familiar with the concept of developing melodies, specifically from a technical aspect. We can simply load up any synth sound and play around with notes until we stumble upon something we like. But, as a producer, your goal isn't to satisfy only yourself. The goal is to fulfill the expectations of the listeners as well as the artist's vision for the project. When you connect these two things, you are creating a satisfying melody.

Here is where you can separate yourself from the rest. A melody has the power to drive the entire direction of a song. Most beat makers don't look at themselves as melody writers. Because the developing of melodies is often random, the assumption is that there isn't strategic approach or process. Since melodies need to be catchy and unforgettable, a producer needs to know how to create melodies under various circumstances. For example, a songwriter may come up with catchy title or hook. It's your job as the producer to build a melody based on that idea. This isn't about creating any melody to pair with the hook. The melody and hook must compliment each other, and be equally as powerful. What if an artist has gone through an experience and wants to turn the idea into a song? As a producer, you must develop a melody that captures that pain and emotion. Instead of randomly looking for beats that may satisfy the feeling, take a leading approach and build a melody on that specific concept in mind.

Of the flip side, as a beat maker or producer, you may have a great melody but face the challenge to build around it. This is where you need to be cautious. A beat maker must be a good decision maker and know when to say when. Don't add so many elements that distract from the melody. If you're able to create a great melody, make sure it's always remains the number one focus. Listeners will remember your melody before the actual lyric. Your goal as a producer is to add all the pieces (elements) without compromising the integrity of the melody. This includes lyrics as well. How many times have you heard someone sing a melody line in a way that sounded awkward? This is because words are being crammed into the melody in an unnatural way. Catchy melodies work when the phrases sound like natural dialogue.

As a simple tip, focus on playing a melody with one hand without adding chords. This forces you to concentrate on playing a sequence of notes. Record as many takes as possible and then listen back. I guarantee you will hear a melody line you can build on. Once you are absolutely satisfied that your melody is original and unforgettable, then add the other elements. Finally, your melody needs to add tension to your song. This is done by creating verse and bridge melody lines that build up to the chorus melody. The chorus melody should be simple and the high point of the range of notes being used.

4.Song Structure
Create effective song arrangement

The musical elements incorporated into a song often dictate the song structure of a song. To make a song more appealing to the listener, songwriters divide songs into sections. Most beat makers begin with a structure built around one sequenced pattern or section. For example, a one four-bar sequence in 4/4 *time signature, which is repeated throughout the song. This tends to create fatigue and bore the listener. The repetitiveness can get overwhelming because as a listener, you instinctively want to hear something change over time.

A producer knows how to create a musical roadmap for the listener to follow. This is done by developing a song structure with the appropriate section. Song structure is important because it organizes our ideas within a song. Just like a movie director, a producer can decide which sections of a song work best to entertain the listener. There are three common song structures that are typically used in popular music today. See below:

Song Structure One: Verse / Chorus / Verse / Chorus / Bridge / Chorus
Song Structure Two: Verse / Pre-Chorus / Chorus / Verse / Pre-Chorus / Chorus / Bridge / Chorus
Song Structure Three: Verse / Bridge / Verse

Song structure is much more than just organizing sections in a specific order. A beat maker must understand the purpose of each section and what role it plays within a song. If you know how each section works, you know how to create an effective song structure. Let's start with the ***Verse*** section. This section moves the song forward, especially lyrically. Because the chorus repeats the same elements, the verse introduces new ideas and moves the song forward in one direction. The ***Chorus*** reflects the main idea or concept. This is the catchiest part of the song. The part of the song that gets stuck in people's head. Most people incorporate the title within the chorus to make it easier for listeners to identify the song as well. With a catchy melody as part of the chorus, the verse can distinguish itself too.

The **Pre-Chorus** section is right before the chorus. This sets the listener up for the catchy melody in the main chorus. Musically, it creates a great build up for the chorus. The **Bridge** takes the listener somewhere else, both musically and lyrically. A beat maker must be cautious when introducing something totally new in this section though. At the same time, this is an opportunity to add something interesting. Lastly, there is the **Hook** section. Oftentimes, the hook and chorus are interchangeably. The hook is the catchiest part of the song but it doesn't necessarily have be part of the chorus. The hook is the element that people remember. A hook works perfect as the first two lines as well.

This is only the basics of song structure. Obviously, there are various ways you can structure your song. As a beat maker transitioning to a producer, you must be familiar with popular song structures and use them as a guide to lay out your music. To put it simply, song structure can turn your basic "beat" into a full-length "song." As a producer, your job is to not only know what elements are needed. You also need to know what elements need to be "left" out. The goal is to assure that each individual element fits perfectly with the other elements.

5.Dynamics
Evoke emotion and feeling

A major component of heat making is having the ability to create "the feeling." "The feeling" are a set of musical characteristics that evoke an emotion in the listener. When a person hears music, he or she enters into a state of mind derived from previous circumstances, mood, situations, or relationships with others. Listeners instinctively want to relate their previous experiences with what they hear. When you hear the first few seconds of a song, your mind immediately categorizes what you hear based on two things: Sound and Feeling.

As a producer, you have the power to control the emotions of your listeners. This can be done on the technical side with recording, mixing and mastering. What does the listener hear through their headphones or speakers? This is part of the "sound" category of a listener's mind. Creating great dynamics involve great sound engineering skills. Where sounds and elements are placed "in the mix" is extremely important to a listener's experience. We'll talk about this some more in the mixing section.

As a beat maker, you need to play on a listener's instincts. How do you want the listener to respond when hear your beat? For example, the foundation of "Boom Bap" Hip-Hop is built on unique drum and snare pattern. This is the identifier. When you hear "Boom Bap," you want to bob your head. Bobbing your head is a kinesthetic cue, a listener's reaction or response to what they're hearing. As a producer, your job is to get the listener to respond involuntarily. If listeners respond by dancing, snapping, tapping their feet or bobbing their head, you know you're onto something. If listeners get the chills, goosebumps, cry or change their attitude, then you are really onto something. This skill develops from observing other people listen to your music. If you don't get any kinesthetic responses, you probably need to go back to the drawing board. Music is all about tapping into emotions. When you play music for others, observe their kinesthetic responses immediately. As soon as the track plays, what happens? What are the kinesthetic responses to the mix? Is the 808 bass drum changing the listener's mood? Is the listener still focus and listening?

6.Coaching (Artist & Musicians)
Manage the process

As a huge basketball fan, I enjoy watching talented players. I also enjoy watching the different coaching strategies. As the producer, you need to work with people and bring them together to deliver the best project possible. This requires good leadership skills. A producer is much like a coach. He or she must manage the process to determine the best possible outcome. There are many aspects of music production that require the assistance of others. Producers provide direction to artists, musicians, engineers and songwriters. Your job as a producer is to communicate your vision to the production team.

Communication in itself is a form demonstrating leadership. As a producer, you need to think with clarity, absurd and express ideas, and share a magnitude of information with others. Effective communication skills do not come naturally for most beat makers. After all, most beat makers today create music by themselves in their home studios. Most communication with others is done online. A producer must be a great listener during the creative process, not only musically but also during personal interaction with collaborators.

Listening is probably the most important skill a producer must develop. Producers make decisions based on what they hear, so its essential that producers know what technical cues to listen out for. There are several cues a producer must evaluate to assure that the final product reaching the highest quality. The basic composition cues such as melody, harmony, lyrics and song form need cohesion. Each element should work together with the purpose of maintaining continuity. We know having a catchy melody is great but where should it be placed in the song? How often should it be heard? Does any of the lyrics alter the melody?

Timing and rhythm set the underlying foundation for a song. One sound or instrument not playing in time with others can offset the entire rhythm. Are all the musicians playing together on time? The tone of the artist must fit the specific genre as well. For example, the roughest of Hip-Hop and the cleanliness of Pop are on two different sides of the spectrum. What should be the appropriate tone for the final product? Finally, a producer needs to identify that special "thing" and make sure it shines throughout the song. The "thing" is the X-Factor that distinguishes the artist from all the rest. What combination of vocals and elements make the track intriguing? A producer must ask him or herself these questions throughout the process.

7.Collaboration
Get help from others

Collaboration is the key to success in any field. Working with others can be a huge benefit for both the beat maker and producer. Most beat makers work independently out of their homes or in small studios. Consequently, collaboration must be initiated by the beat maker to appreciate the value that others can provide. As a producer, you are responsible for delivering the best project possible. If help is required, he or she should find the most effective ways to utilize collaboration.

Collaborating with others give you a chance to build meaningful relationships. People are always looking to collaborate and for opportunities to network. The more people you know, the more people who will know you. Networking and relationships are what truly drive the music industry. When you collaborate with someone new, you create a meaningful impression, which builds a powerful relationship. If the relationship is authentic, it will increase trust and the ability to share useful connections. This gives both collaborators a chance to expand and combine their audiences as well.

Collaborating with others also gives you a chance to learn new things. If you are use to working alone, you may find yourself having the same approach to beat making. You may be creating similar melodies, drum patterns, lyrics and mixes. Working with others may get you out of your comfort zone. With fresh ideas provided by others, you can expose yourself to new concepts and approaches towards music making.

Finally, collaborating with others can help you speed up the production process. Most beat makers aren't formally trained musicians. So, traditional music theory concepts aren't understood as easily to beat makers. For example, a beat maker could benefit from an experienced piano player. He or she will be familiar with different chords and progressions that you can incorporate into your track instantly. Also, collaborating with trained musicians opens up opportunities to contribute to music projects without limited beat making or production skills. As a producer, you will be faced with deadlines, so using collaborators to shorten the length of the production process will possibly save money as well.

8.Mixing (Sonics)
Control what listeners hear

When you want to control what listeners hear, you should ask yourself, "What do I want this recording to sound like?" Clean and bright? Raw and dirty? Modern or vintage? Analog or digital? Using these categories, you can build the foundation for your mix. For example, if you're looking to create a vintage 60's vibe, you may need to mix on vintage analog hardware gear or software that emulates analog gear. You may also want to create a mix specifically for a listener's mood. If the listener wants to relax, creating a warm-sounding mix may be appropriate. It's not enough just to prepare a track for the nigh club based on content alone. You need to create a mix that encourages kinesthetic responses in a party environment. For example, when bass or low frequency sounds are used in a dance song, it increases a listener's adrenaline. Just imagine listening to a EDM song without the feeling of that throbbing kick drum.

As I mentioned in the Dynamics section, Dynamics evoke a feeling in the listener. You will know it by observing kinesthetic cues provided by the listener. The "sound" of your mix will ultimately determine a listener's initial kinesthetic cue. Because mixing is the final phase of the song creation process, it's critical that every element is creatively placed between the speakers. If the first few seconds of your track sound loud and distorted, that may make the listener feel uncomfortable or even annoyed. If the first few seconds of your track are "in the pocket," meaning all the elements work in harmony together, the listener won't be distracted and may crave to hear more.

Vocal placement is extremely critical to the overall mix. The first instinct of most beat makers is to place the vocals "on top" of a mixed instrumental, meaning much of the focus is on the musical elements first. Then, the vocal is added after all the elements sound good together. This approach could potentially cause all sorts of challenges when determining where the vocal should be placed. Where is the vocal placed in comparison to other instruments or elements? Vocal placement can be created in various ways with EQ, reverb or gain. Ask yourself, can I hear each word? Does the vocal sound close or far away? Do the instruments support the vocal? What impact do you want the vocal to have?

Lastly, in this digital age, music lovers are listening to music on mobile devices more than ever before. Consequently, it will be a challenge to create a music mix that translates across multiple mobile and hardware devices in the same way. Do you create mixes for headphones? Built-in speakers? Bluetooth speaker transmission? Music streaming platforms also compress music files to distribute music to consumers. One challenge most mix engineers are faced with is getting low frequency instruments to cut through small speakers. Have you ever tried to hear an 808 bass kick or bass guitar on a mobile device or laptop. One of the simplest techniques you can do is "free up head room." It's the addition by subtraction method. Each element takes up a certain amount of frequency space. By eliminating unused frequency space, you can "free up" and increase frequency space where needed. For example, if you decrease the low frequency filter range of several elements, this will give you room to allow a low frequency sound to stand out in the mix. Applying this simple strategy will approve your mixes dramatically.

Mixing A Song

Here are some quick tips to get you started:

1. **Rough Volume Mix -** Create a mix by adjusting the gain levels of each track. Remember, it's all about how the sounds work together, not separately.
2. **Mix Buss Set-Up -** Once you have a rough mix, create a Buss section. This will allow you to insert

effects on multiple tracks and save time, effort and computer power.

3. **Compression** - This is the difference between creating an average mix and a professional mix. Compression creates power, punch and the energy needed to take your mix to the next level.

4. **EQ** - This is probably the most effective tool. When used correctly, EQ can provide clarity, width and dimension to your mix.

5. **Effects (Reverb & Delay)** - Spice up your mix by creating the room for the listener. After recording your sound clean without distortion, some natural characteristics could get lost. Use Reverb to bring back the feeling of a natural environment.

6. **The Special Sauce** - Put your final touch on the mix by adding your "special sauce," which is the effect that brings the entire mix together. Listen to the mix from start to finish to make sure it sounds like one cohesive piece of art.

9.Creativity
Think outside the box

As a beat maker and creator, your primary focus is to create new forms of art. That's a concept understood by most but it's easier said than done. Similar to a musician of a physical instrument, a beat maker can get complacent and hit a creative wall. Some may refer to this stage as "beat block." This problem doesn't come from your inability to meticulously think of something new. The problem comes from the mental constraints beat makers put on themselves. As a solution, a beat maker must "think outside of the box." The "box" is your mind filled up with the ideas and skills you are use to applying normally. "Thinking outside the box" is the process of developing new ideas that intentionally goes against your common approach.

To start the process, you must first identify what your "comfort zone" is. This can be anything such as your environment, the equipment you use, the date and time your wish to create, who you collaborate with, what type of music you create, sound selection, and more. Choose your top 10 comfort zone areas and use them as your "box" guide. These will be the areas you should approach differently. For example, instead of using your favorite sound kit, simply create your own and commit to using it for a period of time.

Another thing you can do is make conscious assumptions during the beat making process. A conscious assumption is having the ability to predict an outcome based on your actions. For example, instead of recording sounds one by one into a sequence, think about how three or four sounds will work together first. What do you think the outcome would be? What will be the consequences once you put everything together? If you're a chess or card player, this strategy should be familiar to you.

After making assumptions, challenge them. Ask yourself, Why did this work? What if I make some changes? How can I make this work? This is also the stage when you can ask yourself the four WHYs of true success: Why? Why not? Why not I? Why not now? Most of us have ingrained assumptions that help us make decisions but this common knowledge may not be correct. As a producer, you are a catalyst of outside-of-the-box thinking. A producer's job is to question these assumptions to foster creativity. Remember, your previous music knowledge play two opposing roles: it serves as the foundation for new ideas, at the same time it forces out an old way of thinking. Always keep an open mind.

Lastly, step into the shoes of others. As a beat maker, we tend to believe that our perception is all that matters. We hold on to our opinions with hopes of changing the perception of others. As a producer, your job is to think about how others may perceive your music. If you were a music listener, what would you want to hear? How would you like to hear it? If you were an artist, what elements incorporated into the track get you attention? Remember, your perception of the quality of music depends on the position in which you perceive it.

10.Education
Mastering you craft

When we think about education, we often focus on formal education provided by traditional institutions. The traditional education model is linear, meaning we are taught to learn in stages one level at a time. As you complete your highest level of education, it is assumed that you have reached your peak level. If you ever completed any level of formal education, you have probably asked yourself, "What's next?" This doesn't mean formal education doesn't prepare you for the future. I believe a formal education is great for providing a good foundation to "master your craft."

In the book *Mastery*, Robert Greene provides the framework of using life experiences to perfect your craft. There are several areas in which a beat maker can better him or herself along the path to becoming a successful producer. One suggestion Greene makes is to "Discover your calling." Think about all the reasons why music production sparked your interest in the first place. How did you feel when you discovered it? The goal is to recapture that feeling for personal motivation. Ask yourself, "Why am I doing this?" Once you reconnect with your purpose, you need to find your perfect niche. With so much competition, it's easy to get discouraged and not see where you fit in. Instead of trying to "fit in," create your own niche based on your acquired skills and unique experiences. All of us have our own personal niche. With an effective marketing strategy, a beat maker can amplify its personal niche to build its brand.

Experience comes from practicing your skills over time. Acquiring skills is an ongoing process. When you understand this concept, you will understand that building a music career is a process that should be nurtured and respected. With that said, experimentation is necessary, even if it leads to failure. The process of "trial and error" leads you to mastery.

Mentorship is a great way to learn from other and avoid making the same mistakes. A mentor cannot only offer you life lessons, he or she can also help you assess your skill level and accelerate your learning. Choose a mentor who can fulfill your professional needs and provide support you can't get from others. He or she doesn't necessarily need to be an expert in the music field. In most cases, your development will focus in areas of personal weakness and less on your musical talents. Most beat makers struggle with motivation, maintaining confidence and direction. A great mentor can point out your weaknesses and provide feedback that will help you improve. As you learn new concepts, your job is to apply them in your own creative way.

Conclusion

In closing, this book was never intended to be the secret formula for guaranteed results. We have only scratched the surface of the many ways to become a successful producer. Heat making is a process that can be customized to fit your professional needs. Similar to a food recipe, as a beat maker, you can add or subtract the necessary ingredients that work for you. Each technique should be viewed as a focus area for your own self-development. A producer must understand how to develop concepts, play an instrument, create catchy melodies, arrange a song, evoke emotion, control what listeners hear, direct artists and musicians, and deliver a project that is sonically pleasing. Are you ready?

References

Branch, D. (2014). *The beat game: The truth about hip-hop production*. New York, NY: Branch Family Publishing.

Greene, R. (2012). *Mastery*. London, United Kingdom: Penguin Books.

Maxwell, J. (1993). *Developing The Leader Within You*. New York, NY: HarperCollins Publishing.

BRANCH FAMILY
PUBLISHING

www.DarrellBranch.com

Printed by Amazon Italia Logistica S.r.l.
Torrazza Piemonte (TO), Italy

16244408R00018